This book is a work of fiction.
It emerges from the creative mind of Isabella Tirado. All names, characters, places, and events are figments of my imagination or included just for fun. If anything seems familiar, it's purely a happy accident. Enjoy the journey!

Published by: Isabella Tirado
Created and printed in: United States of America

The book was designed and illustrated by me, the author, using digital tools like Canva and AI, based on my imagination, to make the story even more special for you!

Copyright © 2025 by Isabella Tirado
All rights reserved. No part of this book may be copied, stored, or shared in any way—whether digitally, on paper, or otherwise—without asking permission first, except for brief quotes that help me spread my tales to encourage others to discover and buy my books.

The Wish is my first edition, published in 2025. It's part of a series I plan to create after this debut, and I genuinely appreciate your support, buying my Books and sharing your feedback help me grow as a writer.

ISBN: 9798285199502

Thanks so much for reading! I hope you enjoy the adventure as much as I loved writing it. This book is part of my journey of building my own business, with the help of my personal advisor, Blukastor LLC. They're guiding me in growing my story-sharing passion, using my skills and passions, and encouraging me to focus on the future without losing sight of what truly matters today.

The Wish

One wish, many memories lost!

The Aubrey's Tales: A Kid's Journey to Discover, Shine, and Be Your Awesome Self!!

Authors Note!!!!

    This story came from a feeling I didn't expect, something real I've seen in the world. Many kids are judged for things they can't control: their race, how much money their family has, what they believe, or how they live. But I've learned that love is more powerful than all of that. Love can't be bought, no matter how rich someone is. It's something that lives in your heart, not your wallet.

    My mom always reminded me to look at the kids who don't have enough to eat, to have toys or a warm place to sleep. That stayed with me. So I wrote about Aubrey, a girl who didn't have much but had a family that loved her. Even though she was bullied for having less, her heart stayed strong. When she makes a wish, things start to change, maybe for the better or worse.

This story is for anyone who's ever felt left out, different or small.

You are enough. Love matters most.

Isa T

The Wish.
Many Memories lost.

To my parents, sister, and brother.
Thank you for always supporting me, even when all hope feels lost. You guys always help me get back up again.

This Book belongs to:

_____

Table of Content

Chapter 1:
- Aubrey's World

Chapter 2:
- A Penny's Worth of Kindness

Chapter 3 :
- The Mysterious Note

Chapter 4:
- A Flicker of Hope

Chapter 5:
- The Transformation

Chapter 6:
- The Price of a Wish

Aubrey's World

Chapter 1

Aubrey's family was one of the poorest in Scotland. They lived in a small, cramped house where Aubrey, her dad, and her mom squeezed together every night, navigating life's daily struggles with perseverance. Each room felt like a shared heartbeat, pulsing with their hopes and dreams despite the weight of financial burdens pressing down on them.

Aubrey wore torn and dirty clothes, often hand-me-downs or thrift store finds, which she creatively mixed and matched to reflect her unique style. While small for her age, her spirit was incredibly big. She treasured her worn, navy blue backpack, plastered with patches and doodles—a canvas that told her story and held the treasures of her imagination: a notebook filled with ideas and a collection of books that whisked her away to far-off places.

Aubrey's dad worked as a janitor during the day and flipped burgers at McDonald's at night. Her mom could only spare an hour at home for dinner before heading out to clean a nursing home overnight. Despite their financial struggles, Aubrey's parents instilled the importance of education and kindness in their daughter. Every night, they gathered for dinner, sharing stories and laughter that created a feeling of belonging even in their humble surroundings. They encouraged Aubrey to pursue her studies and impart the values of compassion and empathy. It was this nurturing environment that helped Aubrey bloom; she was incredibly smart, always earning A+ grades, and always stood out as the teacher's favorite.

A Penny's Worth of Kindness

Chapter 2

Not every day was easy. On her way to school, Billy approached her, laughing and hurling mean-spirited comments. "Wow, cool outfit! Where's your janitor uniform?" he smirked, while his friends snickered beside him. Aubrey felt the sting of embarrassment as she walked past, the weight of his words lingering like a heavy cloud. Sometimes, she wished she could be "normal" to fit in without the labels that came from her family's financial situation.

After school, as she walked home, Aubrey passed a homeless man sitting quietly by the sidewalk. Feeling a surge of compassion, she fished out a penny from her pocket and handed it to him. "I'm sorry, that's all I have!" she said, her voice filled with sincerity. The homeless man's eyes sparkled with gratitude as he handed her a crumpled note. "Read it when you get home, Aubrey," he said softly. Aubrey felt a strange mix of fear and curiosity, and she hurried away.

The Mysterious Note

Chapter 3

In her living room, Aubrey opened the note eagerly. One side read: "One wish." On the other: "Many memories lost."

"Yeah, right! What a prank," she scoffed, dismissing it with a smile. Just then, the front door creaked open. "I'm home!" her mother called out. Aubrey rushed down to greet her, her excitement bubbling as they began to talk about their day.

"Tell us the weirdest thing that happened today!" her mom encouraged, stirring the pot of soup with a light-hearted grin.

Aubrey chuckled as she recounted her encounter with the homeless man and shared the mysterious note. "Imagine if it were true!" she exclaimed.

"Like if I wished for a lifetime supply of pancakes!" her mom chimed in, laughing. "And I'd wish for a golden toilet seat!" her dad added with a mischievous wink, causing Aubrey to burst into giggles.

"Or I'd wish for a dog that does my homework!" she quipped back, and they all laughed together as they imagined the ridiculous scenarios.

In those moments, the weight of their struggles faded, replaced by the warmth of each other's company and the joy of sharing silly dreams.

A Flicker of Hope
Chapter 4

After eating and finishing her homework, Aubrey slipped into bed, the note still on her mind. The next day, as she daydreamed at school, doubt crept in. "What if it is true? What would I wish for?" she pondered. As she imagined wishing for wealth, a flicker of hope ignited within her.

When she returned home to grab the note, panic surged through her. "No! Where is it?!" she cried, tears brimming in her eyes. After searching every corner of the house, she finally found it crumpled in the trash can. Relieved, she took a deep breath and whispered, "I wish we were wealthy."

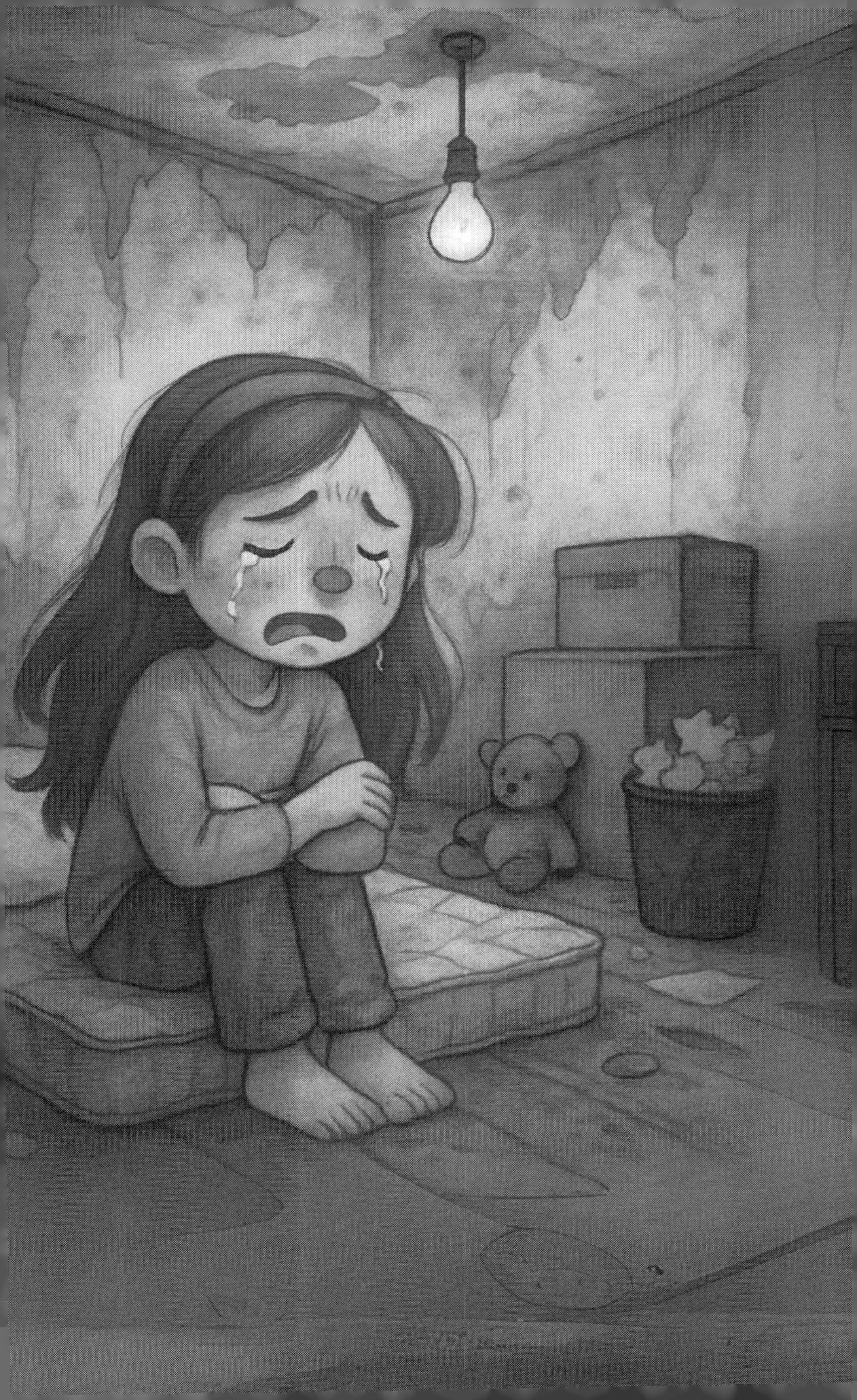

The Transformation

Chapter 5

Suddenly, a magical shimmer enveloped Aubrey, and a voice echoed, "Your wish is my command." Time seemed to pause as her modest living room transformed into a grand hall. The torn couch, now draped in plush white fabric, shimmered with gold accents. Chandeliers sparkled above, and walls adorned with portraits of her family in fancy clothes surrounded her. At first, she marveled at the sight, glancing down at her hands, now adorned with sparkling jewelry. Her clothes were fresh, clean, and stylish. She felt like one of those rich kids at school.

"Aubrey, sweetie! Come downstairs for breakfast!" called her mother's voice, but it sounded different: calm, rested, and cheerful.

She hurried down to find her dad reading a newspaper in a sharp suit and her mom sipping coffee from a golden cup while wearing a beautiful dress. The air was filled with the delicious aroma of pancakes and flowers.

The Price of a Wish

Chapter 6

"Hey... remember when we used to live in that tiny house?" Aubrey asked, trying to connect with her parents. They exchanged puzzled looks as if trying to understand her words. "What tiny house?" they asked, their faces blank.

The laughter and warmth of their small home seemed to fade like a distant memory. She recalled the joy of her parents' laughter, the intimate moments spent together watching movies, and the nights her mom wrapped her in a blanket, whispering, "It'll be okay."

Aubrey looked around at the lavish decor, wealth surrounded her, and felt a heavy weight in her chest. Her heart ached as she pondered what her wish had cost her: the memories and values that had defined who she was and the love that had surrounded her. Those precious memories, the feelings of love and togetherness, were fading from her mind bit by bit. "But now my parents will have more time for me, they will love me, and they won't be exhausted, right?" she thought, tears brimming in her eyes.

Right? The question echoed in her mind, coupled with a sense of uncertainty. Would all of this be as perfect as it seemed? Will everything turn out all right?

As Aubrey sat in her beautifully adorned living room, the realization began to settle in, she had made a choice, but at what cost? The future felt uncertain, and with a heavy heart, she pondered whether their parents would ever need the memories of the love that had shaped them.

Will everything be alright?

The End?
To Be Continued...

TO BE COUNTINUED..

**One Wish
Many Memories
LOST!**

If you enjoyed reading "The Wish," please consider leaving a review on Amazon. Your feedback is my way to grow and also helps other readers discover this story.

Stay tuned for the continuation of Aubrey's journey in the upcoming sequel!

ABOUT THE AUTHOR

Hi there! Want to know a little secret about the person who made this story? Let me introduce myself